Developing Your Character In Creative Writing

For Middle School & High School

Written by:
Stacey Cotrufo

©2011 Stacey Cotrufo

Table of Contents

- Introduction

- Lesson One: What Comes First – Story or Character?

- Lesson Two: The Importance of an Outline

- Lesson Three: Giving Your Character a History

- Lesson Four: Giving Your Character a Voice (Actions & Reactions)

- Lesson Five: A Family Affair

- Lesson Six: Physical Description – What do They See in the Mirror?

- Lesson Seven: How Demographics Shape Who We Are?

- Lesson Eight: A Day in the Life of Your Character

- Lesson Nine: The When & Where of Character Description Placement

- Lesson Ten: Dialogue – Lunch With Your Main Character

- Lesson Eleven: Character Transformation

©2011 Stacey Cotrufo

INTRODUCTION – DEVELOPING YOUR CHARACTER

Welcome to "Developing Your Character in Creative Writing"!

This workbook is designed to help you, young writers, learn the process of developing your characters. You see, it takes more than a great idea or plot to make an interesting story; your characters need to be people that your readers can relate to. Whether your character is a hero, heroine or villain, if developed correctly, your readers will have strong feelings about them.

The workbook will cover these lesson topics:

- What comes first – the story or characters?
- The importance of an outline
- Character identification
- Giving your character a history
- Physical descriptions
- How demographics shape who your characters are
- Giving your character a voice
- A day in the life with your character
- When and where of character description placement
- And so much more!

By the end of this book your character will become a living, breathing, three-dimensional person of your own creation that you will have great ease writing about! Having great characters and knowing them intimately makes writing for them a much easier prospect. And really, as writers, aren't we hoping for our stories to be easier to write?

For today I'll start off with my introduction.

I am a married, mother of two, Indie author and freelance writer from Wake Forest, North Carolina. Her freelance work can be seen on Examiner.com, eHow, Bukisa.com, The Mouse for Less Guest Blog as well as in the Wake Weekly newspaper. I have taught various writing classes to the homeschool community for almost ten years and my classes have included: Creative writing, literary essay writing, research paper writing and more personalized workshops such as dialogue writing and character developing.

©2011 Stacey Cotrufo

Developing Your Character   Introduction – pg. 2

I am currently writing my sixth contemporary romance and have been an active participant in National Novel Writing Month (NaNoWriMo) and Amazon's Breakthrough Novel Award contests and was a top five finalist in the International contest of Harlequin's Editor's Pitch Challenge.

My first Indie published book, "Jordan's Return" came out in November of 2011. My second book, "The Christmas Cottage" was released in November of 2012 and was a best seller on Amazon. My newest release "Ever After" is being released in February of 2013 and I just recently signed a contract for a full length novel with the Seymour Agency in New York.

Writing is a passion of mine and I am excited about my future in publishing!

Take a moment and describe yourself. How would you introduce yourself if you were being interviewed?

_____

_____

_____

_____

_____

_____

_____

_____

©2011 Stacey Cotrufo

How to Use this Book

This curriculum was originally designed as a four-week workshop with the lessons posted on Mondays, Wednesdays and Fridays. With the workbook format, you are free to use this as you see fit and spread out the lessons however you want. Each lesson will require some sort of action by you, the student, but most of the assignments will be brief and easy for you to work on. This was how it was done as an on-line format:

Week #1:
Monday – Introduction
Wednesday – What Comes First – the Story or the Characters?
Friday – The Importance of an Outline

Week #2:
Monday – Giving Your Character a History
Wednesday – Giving Your Character a Voice (Actions & Reactions)
Friday – A Family Affair

Week #3:
Monday – Physical Descriptions: What do they see in the Mirror?
Wednesday – How Demographics Shape Who we Are
Friday – A Day in the Life of Your Character

Week #4:
Monday – The When and Where of Character Description Placement
Wednesday – Dialogue: Lunch With Your Main Character
Friday – Character Transformation

This is just an example of how to divide up the topics. If you want to use the book five days a week, that will work. If you would only like to use the book once a week, that will work too! Being that creative writing is not usually something done as a primary subject, you fit it in to your schedule wherever you see fit.

©2011 Stacey Cotrufo

Developing Your Character   Introduction – pg. 4

HOMEWORK:

As I stated earlier, I believe that you will get the most out of this workbook if you actively participate in the assignments and discussions. With each lesson there will be a homework assignment for you to complete. The purpose of this is for you to put in to practice what we are discussing. If you do all of the exercises and assignments, by the end of the book you will have a solid foundation with your characters to place into your story.

The thing to remember is that when you are writing creatively, there are no right or wrong answers; it is all what you have created in your mind. Share your work with a parent, your family or friends and get their feedback! Don't be ashamed of what you've done, sometimes getting feedback from others enhances the creative process!

Most importantly, just keep writing. Do all of the assignments and whether you do them here in the book or on computer or wherever it is that you feel comfortable, just be sure to get your ideas down on paper. If you need to step away from your work for a day or two, that's okay. Never get discouraged because you can do anything that you put your mind to!

Getting Started!

What type of stories do you like to read? What type of stories do you think you'd like to write? What kinds of characters interest you the most in a story? What kind of character do you most relate to? Take a moment and write that out below. Remember to use full sentences and tell why you enjoy this type of genre.

_____

_____

_____

_____

_____

©2011 Stacey Cotrufo

Developing Your Character   Introduction – pg. 5

©2011 Stacey Cotrufo

WHAT COMES FIRST – THE STORY OR THE CHARACTER?

You've got a great idea for a story…you can picture it all so clearly in your mind. Whether it's general fiction, action/adventure, Sci-fi, western or paranormal, you cannot have a story without great, compelling characters.

The Chicken or the Egg?
This is an age-old question. What came first? Only God knows the answer to that one but for us writers, the answer truly comes down to us. What do I mean by that? Well, sometimes you create a story. You start out with the plot and then plug characters in and their story turns out beautifully. But somewhere in that story is a secondary character who is begging to have a voice – a story of their own. Now you have to figure out how to write a story just for them. So really, it can be done both ways in our creative world but for the sake of this class, we are going to take the stance of the story coming first.

What's Going On?
Most writers always have a story going on in various stages – whether it's in their head or on their computer. A common problem that stalls the story is that they are unsure where they want that particular story to go. What can help us get over that hump (or writer's block) is to know our characters so intimately that we instinctively know what they would do next in any situation that we can create.

A good starting point is to look at the story that you want to tell in simplest terms. By that I mean that you can describe your overall plot in a few short sentences. This process will come in handy much further down the road in your journey to getting published so make sure you write it down!

Example:
Four childhood friends spend one last summer together before one of them gets married. But it's not only the bride-to-be that is facing a whole new life. Over the course of the summer, relationships will change and all four will see their friendships in a whole new light.

©2011 Stacey Cotrufo

Developing Your Character   Lesson One – pg. 7

This is a very rough description of a contemporary women's fiction story that I am working on right now. The general idea here is that it is a rough outline of what I want my story to be about and sometimes that's all we have to start with – a rough idea. Now comes the fun part: Filling in all of the blanks to find out WHO these friends are!

Remember Your W's...
Who? What? Where? Why? Simple, right? Well, all good stories have to answer those four W's. So far we have established (roughly) the what – that is the basic plot of our story. You may, at this point, want to establish the "where" – as in where your story will take place. Believe it or not, this is a fairly important factor and one that we will be discussing in Week 3 when we go over the demographics lesson. Where we come from and where we live makes a difference in who we are and how we behave.

For example: I am originally from Long Island. I was born and raised there and then at the age of 27, we moved to North Carolina. The differences in these two cultures which are both on the East coast of the United States and only five states apart were huge! The accents are different, the fashions were different, the food was different – even after 15 years of living in North Carolina I'm still finding so many contrasts between the two cultures. It's these contrasts that shape the people that we are so knowing where your story is going to take place will help you define a little bit of your character.

Once you have your "what" and your "where" we can finally get to the "who"! Who are the people that are going to tell your story? What makes them the kind of people that you want to write about? What kind of "voice" are they going to have? We are going to flesh them out over the next several weeks so you have plenty of time to think this part through.

A side note for you to consider: Stories can get really confusing when you introduce too many characters. It makes it hard (as the writer) to keep track of everyone's voice but it's even harder for the reader to make sense of it all. For the sake of this workshop, we are only going to focus on TWO main characters and work from there.

©2011 Stacey Cotrufo

Developing Your Character   Lesson One – pg. 8

Final Thoughts...
Remember, we as writers are individuals. There is no right or wrong way to create your story. For the sake of being on the same page we are going to say that for this workshop that the story is going to come first – or the IDEA of the story is going to come first. When you are sitting down and writing your own story it may be different and that is okay.

Remember those three W's to get you started and once you've answered them, you will be on your way!

Exercise 1:
Write out the basic plot line of your story in 1-3 sentences. Then decide where your story will take place. Be sure to decide what kind of story this is that you are going to write: romance, action/adventure, Sci-fi, paranormal, etc. Next, I want you to decide on your two main characters. ONLY two. Give us a very brief description of them: a name and maybe one or two sentences about them.

_____

_____

_____

_____

_____

_____

_____

_____

©2011 Stacey Cotrufo

Developing Your Character   Lesson One – pg. 9

©2011 Stacey Cotrufo

THE IMPORTANCE OF AN OUTLINE

I am a list maker. I love to make out a list of the things that I have to do and then cross them off when I am done. It's a weird habit but it gives me a sense of accomplishment and it keeps me on task. It took me YEARS of writing before I realized that the same principle could be applied to my writing.

November is National Novel Writing Month (NaNoWriMo). The challenge is that you have 30 days to write 50,000 words. The first year that I found out about it, the date was November 1! I already felt behind! There are huge on-line communities and forums dedicated to this challenge and so for those who knew of its existence, they certainly did have a leg up on me!

So off I went to start writing. Luckily, I had a story in my head and happily began typing. My story was flowing, at times I could write 5,000 words in a day and have to force myself to stop – apparently my family wanted clean clothes and food! Somewhere around the 20,000 word point, however, I began to struggle. All of a sudden I was asking myself, "What is my character's last name?", "Did he have green eyes or blue?", and "What kind of car did she drive?"

Small details like this can make you crazy if you have to keep going back through your writings to find the answer! In the case of NaNoWriMo, writers are encouraged to just plow forward with their story and NOT go back and edit or re-read what they've written. The theory is that if you can just GET to the 50,000 word mark (and it is not an easy goal!) in 30 days, you can go back and do your editing later. You see, you can lose valuable time if you keep going back and editing and re-reading when you could be writing. Having to continually go back and find information was a huge time waster.

Hence the outline.

Now I have had students who do a very precise, bullet-point type of list. It's a timeline for their story. That is a great tool to have, for sure. But when dealing when we are in the character development phase, you need a little something more.

©2011 Stacey Cotrufo

Developing Your Character			Lesson Two – pg. 11

We all have a timeline of our lives. For example: You're born. Say at 8 months you started to crawl, at 12 months you were walking, at three years old you were talking in complete sentences, at age five you started kindergarten and so on and so forth. That's not really what we're looking for unless your main character happens to be a baby!

In most cases, our main characters are adults. For those of you in that age category, you know that there are a lot of life experiences that you have had that made you in to the person that you are today and those experiences affect almost everything that we do.

You see, it's not just a physical description that makes for your character's development – although we are going to address that a little later on in more detail – but it is their personalities and actual character that we are going to look at today.

The bio that I gave you in the introduction is mainly focused on the writing part of my life but that is only a small fraction of who I am. I am a wife, a mother, a sister, a daughter. I love to read and cook and I hate to exercise. FYI, NOT a good combination! I enjoy romantic comedies in movies and sitcom comedies on TV; I loathe documentaries and sitting out in the sun on a summer day makes me absolutely crazy.

I had open heart surgery when I was four, broke my collar bone at the age of four and slipped and fell on the ice when I was 13 and broke my ankle. I wore braces for four years and glasses and now wear contacts.

I love anything chocolate and despise fruit. Steak and Chinese food are favorites of mine and I don't like pizza. My parents were in the food business with delis all of my life and my sister has a catering business. I chose to go in to retail and then education and office work. I'm a jack of all trades.

I have the gift of hospitality and I love to socialize and talk to people. My friends mean the world to me and after 23 years of marriage, my husband is still my best friend.

©2011 Stacey Cotrufo

So what do you get out of all of that random information? What kind of person does that make me? If you were using these traits for your character you would not find me working in a library or lawyers office! I wouldn't be a vegetarian or working in a science lab.

I think that what my character traits say is that I am a friendly, sociable person who loves to be around other people. I'm not a health-nut so you won't find me at the gym (although I am continually agonizing over my weight!). I'm not overly clumsy and I love to laugh. I am a person deeply committed in all of my relationships and I do have a family.

Random events from our lives also come out in who we are. There are fears and phobias that we all have. For some it could be heights or the fear of the water. For some men it's fear of commitment! We all have them and they don't make us weak, they make us more relatable. Even Indiana Jones, the ultimate man who seemingly could do anything was afraid of snakes! Let your character have them, too! It will strengthen them, not weaken them.

Exercise 2
First, I want you to write up a brief outline of your story. Just hit the high points. You can do this as a bullet-point list or as a paragraph depending on what you are more comfortable with.

Next, I want you to give a brief outline of your two main characters. Who are they? Where are they from? Give a short physical description and any important information that you think we need to know up front. We will do a more detailed history of them later on in the book so for now, keep your descriptions short and to the point while our characters start to take shape.

_____

_____

_____

©2011 Stacey Cotrufo

GIVING YOUR CHARACTER A HISTORY

We all have a history. We have lived many years, had things happen to us, we've traveled places, we've met people, taken classes, learned different skills...we have life experiences that make us the people that we are today.

No two people, not even twins, share the same history. Yes, within a family you may have similar traits, looks, characteristics; you may have travelled to the same places and learned the same things, but our interactions with people are what truly can shape the people that we are. Being able to identify with some of these things can help you with your character and then help you with your story.

For example, let's take this story of two sisters. They are three years apart in age. Sister number one was born in 1965. She was a friendly baby, happy toddler and loved to sing and dance. Sister number two was born in 1968. She was not a happy baby; she cried a lot and was painfully shy. Sister number one was fiercely independent while sister number two preferred to sit back and watch others. Sister number one was always healthy, while sister number two had some major medical issues that required surgery, medication and constant doctor appointments up until the age of 12.

Now, while they were both born and raised on Long Island, both travelled to Florida several times with their parents, both learned to work in their parents business, they were very different people.

Do you have siblings? If so, think about the differences between you. You see, living in the same house does not give you the same life experiences. You've had different friends, different hobbies, different teachers in school, etc. Having the same parents does not make you replicas of one another. As you get older you will learn to understand even the differences you may have with your siblings in the relationships you have with your parents.

Think about your story. While your story may take place during a very short period of your character's life, there is a reason why they are the person that they are and as the creator of that character, you get to decide exactly what those reasons are! How cool is that?

©2011 Stacey Cotrufo

Developing Your Character   Lesson Three – pg. 15

What makes someone turn into a villain? What makes someone painfully shy? What could have happened in someone's past to make them have the powerful urge to succeed while others have no ambition? You see, it is the things that happen to us while we are growing up, combined with genetics, that shape us in to the adults we become.

What makes for a superstar athlete? Why does someone aspire to rise above poverty while others cannot? What gives someone the desire to become a Christian and know God while others do not? Why can some people cook and others can't?

Some of these questions are simple to answer, others are not. For me, I learned to cook because my parents were in the food business my whole life. I sort of had no choice BUT to learn how to cook. Because I was exposed to it so early in life, I am comfortable in the kitchen. My grandmother's both loved to cook and I would cook meals with them. Other people have not been exposed to that kind of upbringing and so cooking is a challenge and not something that they enjoy.

We cannot always choose the type of person we turn out to be, some things are just born in to us (or not). I cannot sing. No matter how badly I want to, I just cannot carry a tune. We all don't have the same talents and that's a good thing! Diversity in the kind of people we are is what makes our relationships interesting. It would be a pretty boring world if we were all exactly the same!

So back to your character…what kind of person are they? Quiet? Outgoing? Bold? Comical? Mean? Selfish? Giving? This is where you get to have fun. You get to create someone essentially since birth. You can describe what sort of things have happened in their lives, what kind of family they come from. You do not have to make this in to a novel itself. Most of the history that you give them may never be mentioned in your story in any great length, but for YOU the writer to really understand them, you are going to have to create and know what makes these people tick. Are you up for the challenge?

©2011 Stacey Cotrufo

Developing Your Character   Lesson Three – pg. 16

Exercise 3:
In this exercise you are going to take ONE character and give a detailed history of their life. Some of things you can include are:
- How old are they?
- Where are they from?
- Do they have siblings?
- How big is their family?
- What are some of their likes and dislikes and why?
- A brief physical description
- Give them at least ONE traumatic incident from their childhood
- Who influences them and why?
- What is their job/career? (if they are an adult)
- What are their hobbies? Talents?
- Give them at least one embarrassing moment
- What is their highest education and what did they study?
- What is their relationship like with their best friend?
- What are they afraid of?
- What makes them happy?

As an extra challenge, I would love to see you write this a bit more formally. By this I mean that I don't want you to just answer the questions in a bulleted list like this, although doing it that way as well will be an easy reference for you while writing, but I would like you to write it out in paragraph form, as well.

The reason I ask for you to do it both ways is to get you in to the habit of writing your paragraphs and keeping each paragraph limited to a specific topic or point of interest. That means writing a life history will be more than one paragraph for sure. Take your time and think it through and introduce me to a well thought out character.

©2011 Stacey Cotrufo

Developing Your Character

Lesson Three – pg. 19

©2011 Stacey Cotrufo

Developing Your Character   Lesson Four – pg. 20

Giving Your Character a Voice
(Actions & Reactions)

As we discussed in lesson three, we all have a history. The things that happen to us in our life make us into the people that we are. It is those events along with (again) genetics that make us speak, act and respond the way that we do in any given situation.

Here's something funny to think about: Imagine that you are having a conversation with your best friend. You are telling them something exciting that happened to you and they sat facing you, back straight, arms at their side, a blank expression on their face and said in a very monotone voice "That's nice."

It would be a bizarre thing to witness, wouldn't it? That's because whenever we talk to another person, we become fairly animated. No one really sits one hundred percent still, with no facial reaction and no voice inflection while talking to another person. It doesn't matter if the person is right there in front of you or on the phone, we move, we laugh, we smile, we yell, we raise our voices, we whisper…there are hundreds of options as to how we act or react while in conversation with other people.

Along those lines, your character is going to have to have those actions and reactions, as well. If you have ever read a book (and I know you have!), whenever you read a scene with two people in it, every sentence does not end with "he said" or "she said". That would make for a completely tiresome story. Different sentences are said with different emotions and you have to sometimes let the reader know what those emotions are from time to time.

Statements like "She exclaimed" or "he yelled" or "she said as she slammed the door" – there is action going on and simply writing "She said" doesn't cover it. Don't (and this is a big DON'T) put action and emotion at the end of every sentence either. That can make for painful reading, too. As a writer, you should be able to get across what is going on in the scene with your characters and their emotions without having to point it out that way.

©Stacey Cotrufo

Developing Your Character   Lesson Four – pg. 21

We will deal with dialogue in greater detail in week four but it is important for you to be thinking about it a little bit now, too. What our main focus today is about how your character(s) act or react in general.

Does your female character twirl her hair? Does your character stutter? Are they nervous? Do they have any sort of OCD behavior? Do they speak softly or are they loud and boisterous? Are they reserved? Happy? Angry? Are there any patterns of behavior that you want to have for them?

Patterns of behavior are kind of a funny thing. Some of us are creatures of habit. We wake up at the same time every day and go about a routine that we repeat day in and day out. We are predictable. Is that how you want your character to be?

Is your character somebody who thrives on taking risks and dangerous situations? Do they enjoy mountain climbing or bungee jumping? Are they patient or impatient? Can they sit down and enjoy a good book or do they have to be on the move all of the time?

It's these traits and actions that will help you figure out how they will respond/react in the situations that you put them in to. For example: If your character is a quiet and reserved person who enjoys sitting down with a good book, chances are they are not impatient and loud! A person with obsessive compulsive tendencies is not going to be spontaneous and willing to go out and put themselves in a risky situation.

And then there is quite literally their voice. How do they speak? I have a pretty heavy New York accent. Living here in North Carolina, I am surrounded by people with Southern accents. I am a loud talker and a loud laugher. Some people speak quietly and would never be seen just laughing out loud. I have been known to speak my mind (only to those that I am extremely comfortable with) while at other times I keep my opinions to myself and let things stay bottled up.

©Stacey Cotrufo

Developing Your Character					Lesson Four – pg. 22

These kinds of actions are important in a character because if your character is confrontational but somewhere along the line learns to be a little bit more reserved and controlled, that would make for interesting character development. It shows a great contrast and we would see the transformation in your story.

We don't respond the same way to the same things all the time. Sometimes, even when you are a happy and outgoing person, you can have a bad day. Even the nicest of people can get grumpy from time to time. Let your character show that human side! They don't have to be happy (or sad) all of the time. Make them be people that are like the people that you know. That will make them more relatable for your reader and make for a more enjoyable story to read.

Exercise Four
Okay, there are two parts to this assignment. First I want you to go and have conversations with at least two different people, separately. For example, have a conversation with your mom and then maybe one with a friend. I want you to observe closely the way that you both interact with one another. Smiles, movement, hand gestures, eye contact, etc. I talk a LOT with my hands and so if you were observing me, you couldn't miss the waving actions! Take notes of the kinds of actions you observed.

The second part of your assignment is to write about your main character and give us a closer look at their voice/actions/reactions. Tell how you see them reacting just in general conversations and life and if you are planning on having them experience any kind of transformation over the course of your story.

If you are a people-watcher, this could be a fun assignment. Someone might think that it's odd that you are watching them so closely but don't let it stop you. It's all for the sake of learning.

©Stacey Cotrufo 2011

Developing Your Character   Lesson Four – pg. 23

©2011 Stacey Cotrufo

Developing Your Character **Lesson Four – pg. 25**

A Family Affair

We all come from somewhere. That's the reality. We all grow up with people around us and whether they are our biological family or not, they affect our lives.

I grew up with a mother, a father and one sister. My parents divorced when I was ten. My dad remarried first; I was seventeen and I gained a step-brother from that marriage. My mom remarried when I was nineteen and I gained three step-brothers and one step sister from that marriage. My once small family was suddenly quite large.

I don't have a lot of cousins, six I think, and we were all close while growing up but as adults, not so much. I can remember sleep-over's and holidays spent together and the memories always make me smile. When I got married I gained three sisters-in-law and their husbands plus seven nieces and nephews. My family continues to grow.

Okay, so now that you're all probably thinking "Well, great for you! Glad to know your family history but what does this have to do with the lesson?" I'll tell you; these people, the people who make up our family, are just another piece of the puzzle that shape who we are.

Basically I grew up with one sibling; my best friend was an only child. Even though we were the same age with the same interests, we were completely different based on the fact that she was an only child. Think about your own family. Do you have siblings? One? Two? More? Are you an only child? Think about your friends? Do they have siblings? Now think about the relationships between siblings whether it's your own or your friends. Do they always get along? Are they competitive or are the confidants?

©2011 Stacey Cotrufo

Developing Your Character   Lesson Five – pg. 27

I think that most of us will agree that while growing up, our relationship with our siblings can be quite rocky. There are fights, teasing, territory issues…the list is endless but at the end of the day we know that while we may not like our siblings, we certainly do love them.

If someone is the oldest sibling, research has shown that they tend to more responsible. The youngest sibling, in contrast, is usually babied a bit more (particularly if part of a larger family) and therefore tends to be a little more spoiled. Birth order can play a large role in the person we turn out to be.

This is part of what Wikipedia has to say on the subject:

"Birth order is defined as a person's rank by age among his or her siblings. Birth order is often believed to have a profound and lasting effect on psychological development. This assertion has been repeatedly challenged by researchers, yet birth order continues to have a strong presence in pop psychology and popular culture.

…Firstborns are "dethroned" when a second child comes along, and this may have a lasting influence on them. Younger and only children may be pampered and spoiled, which can also affect their later personalities. Additional birth order factors that should be considered are the spacing in years between siblings, the total number of children, and the changing circumstances of the parents over time."

While no one theory is 100% correct, it does give us something to think about. So again, what does all of this have to do with our characters? Well, their family history is part of who your character is and can affect how they think and behave.

Competitive sibling relationships will usually carry over in to someone's other relationships and if your character has a sibling where there is that rivalry, chances are that trait is going to come out in other areas of their life. Siblings who are raised as equals and encouraged to love one another without envy or rivalry will grow in to the kind of adults who treat others fairly, as well.

©2011 Stacey Cotrufo

Developing Your Character   Lesson Five – pg. 28

Along with birth order, taking a quick look at the age between siblings can also help define your character. Siblings who are maybe two years apart tend to be closer and have more in common than siblings who are eight years apart.

Traumatic events involving one sibling can also have an effect on the family dynamics and sibling relationships. For example (and I apologize for using myself again!): I was born with a hole in my heart. This was not discovered until I was four years old. At that time my whole family was turned upside down because of it. I had major heart surgery at a time when there was not a good survival rate for such a procedure.

Obviously, I survived just fine but it is a time in my family's life that we all remember quite clearly and that my sister resented because of all of the attention that I required. She was young, too, and didn't understand the severity of the situation but she knew that she did not like having to stay with grandparents or watch as I got piles of presents. If only she knew I would have traded places with her if I had the opportunity!

Losing a parent or a sibling can be devastating no matter what the age. Whether it's due to sickness or an accident or something horrific, a death in the family causes a pain that never quite goes away and can really shape a person. If a boy loses his father, others may turn to him to be the "Man of the House" whereas if the death were that of the mother, daughters would be looked at to fill some of that role.

In the case of the loss of a parent, particularly at a young age, you miss out on that bond and that can be carried with you in to adulthood and you can find yourself searching for someone to fill that void. With the loss of a sibling, it has been said that the surviving children find themselves dealing with a sense of guilt – no matter what the cause of the death. They feel guilty for still being alive when their brother/sister is not and sometimes a grieving parent can make them feel that way.

Kind of depressing, isn't it?

©2011 Stacey Cotrufo

Developing Your Character   Lesson Five – pg. 29

So what kind of family does your character come from? Big or small? Are they the oldest? Youngest?   Any traumatic family events? Do they have a good relationship with their parents? With their siblings? Is there a family business that they are a part of or pressure to be a part of one? Are they competitive or laid back?

Exercise 4:

Tell us about your character's family history. Be creative but realistic. Don't feel like you have to be over the top. If you know the direction that you want your story to go, don't feel like you have to change it to include some of this information but rather fill in the blanks about your characters family from what you already know about them.

Write a good, solid paragraph (or more!) detailing your character's family history and how it has made them in to the person that they are at the time of your story.

_____

_____

_____

_____

_____

_____

_____

_____

_____

©2011 Stacey Cotrufo

Developing Your Character					Lesson Six – pg. 31

Physical Descriptions: What do They See in the Mirror?

When you look in the mirror, what do you see? More specific than just saying "Myself", how would you describe the face looking back at you? Brown hair, brown eyes, round face, freckles…sure, that would be an accurate description for some but not every person with brown hair and brown eyes looks the same. There has to be *more.*

I once read a book where the main female character was described as having a heart-shaped face. That was a lovely description…the first three times it was mentioned. By the tenth time, it felt very repetitive, an unnecessary description to keep using and just plain annoying.

Some things to include in a physical description include: Eye color, hair color, skin tone, face shape, height, build and anything that is obvious about someone's appearance. Do they wear glasses? Do they wear a certain type of clothing? Is their hair style something out of the ordinary or do they wear a hat or some sort of hair accessory that makes them easy to identify? Is their hair curly or straight? Do they wear a certain type of jewelry that stands out when you see them? How do they walk?

Sometimes a physical description of someone isn't always *just* about the physical. We can draw on what we talked about in lesson four (Giving Your Character a Voice) when we describe them. For example, when we describe someone and we get past that initial "What do they look like" phase, we can go in to some of their other traits like how they talk or how they gesture, that sort of thing. Keep that in mind when thinking of their overall description.

Depending on the type of book that you are writing, there isn't always something so obviously outstanding about someone's appearance. If you've read the Harry Potter series, you know that Harry had a lightning strike scar on his forehead. That was something that you surely wouldn't miss and if someone asked you what Harry Potter looked like, you wouldn't have to say more than "He's a boy with dark hair, glasses and, oh yeah, a lightning strike scar on his forehead" and everyone would know what you were talking about.
©2011 Stacey Cotrufo

Most of us don't have something that obvious or remarkable about ourselves or something about our physical attributes that would make us stand out that much in a crowd. Don't think that you have to go over the top with how your characters look. Most of us are pretty ordinary looking but it is what is on the inside that counts. Ordinary is fine. Ordinary is great. BUT (and I emphasize this) you will need to think beyond the "brown hair, brown eyes" description.

There is a way to state things that can make it sound more interesting, as well. For example, not everyone with brown hair has plain brown hair. You can use phrases like "rich brown", "mahogany", "chestnut", "light brown", "dark brown", etc. The same can be said with eye color – it's not always cut and dried on what shade of color someone's eyes are. Blue eyes come in many different shades and the more specific you write, the more your reader will be able to clearly picture your character in their minds as they read your stories.

Exercise Six:
Again, this exercise has several parts. First, I want you to look at this description.

Girl. Blonde hair, blue eyes. Tan and thin. Five feet two inches tall, medium build.

This would be a GREAT description if she was wanted by the police and they just wanted the basics. But you are writing a great story about an interesting character. How can you improve on that description so that she jumps off the page? Re-write the description in more detail that flows.

Next, I want you to look in the mirror and write a physical description of yourself. What do you see when you look in the mirror?

And finally, what does your main character look like? What makes them stand out? If you had to give a thorough description of them to a sketch artist, how would you describe them?

©2011 Stacey Cotrufo

Developing Your Character Lesson Six – pg. 33

Three descriptions. Don't rush it. Take your time and think it through. Look at pictures in magazines. Look at family photo albums. Look at the physical traits that make us look different from everyone else.

_____

_____

_____

_____

_____

_____

_____

_____

_____

_____

_____

_____

_____

_____

Developing Your Character Lesson Six – pg. 34

©2011 Stacey Cotrufo

Developing Your Character   Lesson Seven – pg. 35

How Demographics Shape Who We Are

East coast, west coast. North, South, Yankee or Southerner. Right side of the tracks, wrong side of the tracks. City or suburbs. House or apartment? Public school, private school, home school? Believe it or not, all of these things factor in to the type of people we are.

If you were born and raised in the same home, the same town and never experienced life anywhere else then some of this may be a revelation for you. Where you live, where you grew up plays a big part in the person you are.

For example: I grew up on Long Island. The island itself is not very large. I mean, it is *long* (about 120 miles) but not very wide (about 20 miles). I lived in the middle of the island and had the opportunity to live on both "coasts". Now remember, it's an island. There shouldn't be that much diversity, but there was.

The North shore had a lot more exclusive neighborhoods – a lot of wealthy people, whereas the South shore had more middle class. The North shore had a larger Jewish population than there was on the South shore. That's not to say that there weren't wealthy people on the South shore or no Jewish people on the South shore but you saw more of it on the North side.

Wealth, income, jobs, religion…these things can shape communities. You don't often see a wealthy community that has large mansions and mobile homes side by side. In some cities, neighborhoods are divided by cultures and religions. Our world is a fascinating place to live in but in some ways we are still very segregated.

When we moved from Long Island to North Carolina, I was shocked by the differences. Not only did we *sound* different but the foods were different, the fashions were slightly different, the schooling was different, the climate was different…it was amazing. And it wasn't only the way we sounded that was different it was phrases and words that were different. Up North, you would never address someone as "Miss Stacey"; up there I was either Mrs. Cotrufo or just plain Stacey. That took a little getting used to.

©2011 Stacey Cotrufo

Developing Your Character

When you are creating your character and deciding where they live and where they grew up, you are going to need to research that area so that your character stays true to form. Someone who grew up in the South is going to have a Southern accent and going to say things like "Y'all" whereas a New Yorker would *never* say such a thing. Someone from Brooklyn, New York would have a very specific type of accent and mannerism that you aren't going to find in Nashville, Tennessee.

Someone who grew up with great wealth would carry themselves a bit differently in manners, etiquette and education than say someone who grew up very poor. These are things to look at and consider.

Researching a specific country, state, city, town, etc. can really make your character come alive. Knowing the dialect, the average income and family size is something that will truly help you develop a well-rounded character.

Think about your own family. Where did your parents grow up? How about your grandparents? It is only a small percentage of the population where multiple generations have stayed in one spot. We tend to move around a lot. I was born and raised on Long Island but had moved a total of 12 times in 25 years! For the most part I stayed in a 20 square mile radius but before me, my parents lived more westward on the island. Now I'm in North Carolina, my dad is in Florida while my mom and sister stayed on the island.

It seems with each generation, we move a little bit more and families don't stay as close together geographically as we used to. This is not a bad thing; it kind of introduces different cultures and ways of life to use even if we never leave the United States!

If you grew up in a warm climate and then moved to Minnesota, that would made a huge impact on you and would take a while to get used to. If you grew up on a farm in the country and then moved to New York City, you would have a tough time adjusting. A family of four living in a 3,000 square foot home would live much differently than a family of four living in a 1,000 square foot apartment.

©2011 Stacey Cotrufo

Developing Your Character   Lesson Seven – pg. 37

Change is a good thing. Learning about other cultures is a good thing and while writing about what you know and are comfortable with is easy, doing a little research to help you create an amazing character can be a great experience.

Exercise 7:
Okay, this assignment is going to take you a little bit longer than previous ones. I want you to first research the town that you live in right now. Get the basic demographic facts and any other interesting facts you can find about it and the kind of people that live there. Then I want you to do the same for the place that your parents grew up and then where your grandparents grew up.

Once you have done that kind of research, think about your main character. Where are they from? Where are they at at the time of your story? Some information that I want you to include (and you can write it up as a bullet-point list or in paragraph form, whichever you are more comfortable with):
- Where were they born?
- What is their nationality? (Italian, German, American, etc.)
- Are the wealthy, poor or middle class?
- Where do they live now?
- Tell me about the town?
- Any particular traits, characteristics about where they live?
- Any interesting facts about where they live?
- What kind of home do they live in?
- Make sure to name the city and state where they live
- Make sure you have some geographical knowledge of where they live

©2011 Stacey Cotrufo

©2011 Stacey Cotrufo

Developing Your Character   Lesson Eight – pg. 41

A Day in the Life of Your Character

Okay, today we are going to do some serious writing. Brace yourselves!

Whether you are two, twenty-two or sixty-two, there are things that you do to fill up your day. Some of us are creatures of habit who have a routine that we follow each and every day where others are more laid back and sort of go with the flow. Either way, the average person is awake for approximately 16 hours a day. That is a lot of time to fill.

Some things that we do are necessary – school, work, eating, sleeping, while others are maybe silly or frivolous – watching TV, playing video games, talking on the phone.

Your character lives in a world of your creating. They are real people who have real lives. While your story is not being told in real time and you are not going to write about each and every minute of each and every day of your story's timeline, it is still helpful for you to get as familiar with your character as possible. What do they do with themselves all day?

If your main character is a student, a large portion of their day is taken up with school, chores, homework, socializing with friends. If your main character is an adult, they have a job, they have to commute to work, take care of a family or possibly just themselves.

Most of my days are pretty similar. Here's an example of a typical day:

At 6:15 a.m. my alarm goes off. Not wanting to get out of bed yet, I reach for the TV remote and turn on the morning news. At 6:30, I go and wake up Michael for school. If he's not out of the bed by 6:35, I call him. Sometimes I have to call him several times to make sure he's awake and if there's time, he comes and sits in bed with me and watches a little bit of the news.

©2011 Stacey Cotrufo

Developing Your Character   Lesson Eight – pg. 42

By 6:45, Michael is getting ready for school while I finish watching the news. Once "Good Morning America" starts, I know it's time to start waking up my husband because he's the one that is going to drive Michael to school. He's really difficult to wake up and it takes a solid twenty minutes before he is up and out of the bed. By that time I have gotten out of the bed and started getting Michael's book bag packed and lunch made; sometimes I will have already checked my e-mails.

When Frank and Michael leave at 7:30, I finish checking e-mails, maybe play a couple of games of Scrabble on Facebook and then go and make up my bed. I don't have anyplace to be until noon and I enjoy the quiet time being alone in the house.

If it's a Monday morning, I'll call my sister up in New York and we'll chat for about an hour; other mornings I'll put a call in to my mom or a friend. Unfortunately, 10:00 comes too quickly and then it's time to get in the shower and start getting ready for work. By 11:00, I have to eat lunch and by 11:45 I have to leave for the office.

None of that is particularly exciting but it makes up my day. I'd go in to detail about my job and who I saw and spoke to, the things that I did between the hours of 12 and 5 and then how when I got home I change in to something comfy before starting to cook dinner. We eat together as a family, hang out, I do some writing, play some more Facebook Scrabble, watch some TV…and on and on it goes.

Think about your main character. Student or adult? What does their "typical" day look like? I want to see the details. What time do they get up and why? How long does it take them to get ready for work or school? If they are a student what subjects are they studying? Who are their friends? Their teachers? What activities are they involved in?

What do they do after school or work? Any hobbies that they enjoy while relaxing? What chores do they have? What is their home routine? There are tons of little things that make up our day and we want to hear all about your character's day! Fun, right?

©2011 Stacey Cotrufo

Developing Your Character   Lesson Eight – pg. 43

Be realistic about times and places and the amount of things that can fit into a person's day. Also, remember, we are almost always doing something. No one just sits and stares at the walls so make sure that your character isn't doing a whole lot of that! We want interesting characters to read about – characters that are relatable. Keep that in mind as you make up their day. When in doubt, think about your own day.

Exercise 8:
In detail, write about a day in the life of your main character. From the time they wake up until the time they go to sleep, what makes up their day. Remember, this is not something that I want summed up in a list, timeline or a few sentences. Write this up as detailed paragraphs and really show your creative writing style.

_____

_____

_____

_____

_____

_____

_____

_____

_____

_____

©2011 Stacey Cotrufo

The When and Where of Character Description Placement

So you created this character. You know everything about them – what they look like, what they sound like, what they like to do, how they spend their days. Believe it or not, that was the easy part! This next step will challenge your writing skills and really make you think about where all of that information is going to fit in to your story.

For example, this description showed up on page eight and nine of a book I just finished:

"She did a quick memory check. She'd been out for dessert with friends from work when she met him. They'd talked for a long time. She was an emergency room nurse, he was a paramedic – they'd never met before but she did a lot of business with the fire department and had come to think of them as the good guys."

Up until this point, there has not been one physical description of either of the characters. This is the first glimpse into the people that we are dealing with. The fact that she is an emergency room nurse will end up playing a huge role in the story so this is important information to have right off the bat. The physical description of this character – Cassie – is introduced a bit more slowly over the course of the first 185 pages of this 408 page book.

The reader does not need all of the information right away at the beginning of the story. Sometimes it's nice to disperse the information throughout the book. The only time I would say that you would want to put as much physical description in one paragraph or at one time is if someone is intently *looking* or *staring* at your character and describing what they see; otherwise give the reader glimpses of what they look like.

Another example of a brief glimpse in to the overall character is this:

"In her thick socks, flannel pants, and sweatshirt she climbed the stairs to transform herself from tired pj-clad, Pop-Tart addict into sophisticated wedding photojournalist."

©2011 Stacey Cotrufo

Developing Your Character　　　　　　　　　　Lesson Nine – pg. 47

Here's another:

> *"Emma's dark, shiny hair tumbled under the white lace. Her eyes sparkled a deep, deep brown as she sniffed the weed bouquet. She was tanned, sort of all golden, Mac thought, and scowled at her own milk white skin.*
> *The curse of a redhead, her mother said, as she got her carroty hair from her father. At eight, Mac was tall for her age and skinny as a stick, with teeth already trapped in hated braces.*
> *She thought that, beside her, Emmaline looked like a gypsy princess."*

In those few short sentences we have a pretty accurate picture of these two little girls playing dress up and how they look; the "beautiful" princess and the carrot-top.

Each of the examples gives us just a small part of what makes these characters up but gives the reader just enough information that they can start to form a picture. In the first example, Cassie, all we know in the beginning (and not until page 8) that she is an ER nurse. That information had me picturing her in scrubs but I have no idea of what she physically looked like until much later in the story. The writer focused more on her personality and her relationships rather than on her looks.

Similarly, in the second example, this character's physical description was briefly given in the prologue but it was what she was like as a child. The first chapter focused more on the character's profession, her home, her morning routine before ever mentioning what she looks like now as an adult.

This is a hard thing to decipher as a writer. You have all of this wonderful information about a character that you created so completely and unsure of where to place it. What's more, we won't be able to do it all here in this little workbook because that would mean submitting your entire story and having it all written so that we can all offer our opinions and suggestions. That's not going to happen, right? So what do we do?

©2011 Stacey Cotrufo

Developing Your Character   Lesson Nine – pg 48

First, there is no right or wrong way to do this. If you are comfortable with describing your character on the first page, then you should do it. The funny thing about us writers is that the editing process is never done. You can write your entire story, and feel comfortable that you are writing something awesome and then when it is finished go back and read and think "What in the world was I thinking when I wrote this?"

Don't over think things when you are writing your first draft; chances are you are going to change it later on. You may introduce your character with a full physical description on page three and then somewhere around page 80 realize that you need to do it again. And you know what? THAT'S OKAY! Why? Because the more you go back and read what you've written you will find ways to either re-work it, re-word it or just plain eliminate it. So in the beginning, go with what feels right to you. Remember, this is YOUR story; YOU are the writer. Editors and teachers can make suggestions to you on how something might be "better" worded but at the end of the day, this is YOUR work. If you don't think that something needs to change, then don't do it.

Exercise 9:
Okay, here's another chance to show us your writing style. We are going to experiment with different descriptions and how to work them in to your story.

First, I want you to open your first chapter with a full-on physical description of your character. Even if your first chapter doesn't start this way, I want you for the sake of this exercise to pretend that it does. It should play out that your main character enters a room and someone is watching them (not "Creepy" watching them but as if they just got home and walked through the front door and someone was in the living room watching TV and saw them come in). What does this person sitting on the sofa see? Write the intro from that person's point of view.

©2011 Stacey Cotrufo

Developing Your Character

Next, I want you to come up with several "glimpses" of your character similar to the first and second example I gave at the beginning of the lesson. Something that really doesn't have a whole lot to do with your character's physical description but more of an over-all look at who they are.

And finally, if you are up to it, start a rough draft of the first chapter of your story with some of these things incorporated in to it. I know that is a lot of writing but if you are up to the challenge, this is a great time to see you putting into practice what we have talked about within your actual story.

_____

_____

_____

_____

_____

_____

_____

_____

_____

_____

_____

_____

©2011 Stacey Cotrufo

Developing Your Character······················Lesson Nine – pg. 50

Developing Your Character   Lesson Nine – pg. 51

Developing Your Character　　　　　　　　Lesson Nine – pg. 52

©2011 Stacey Cotrufo

Developing Your Character Lesson Nine – pg. 53

©2011 Stacey Cotrufo

Dialogue: Lunch with your Main Character

One of the best ways to get to know somebody is to sit and talk with them one on one. Sure, you could be introduced to someone at a party or at some sort of event but you don't really get to find out who they are on a deeper level until you actually sit and talk with them in a more relaxed atmosphere.

Like over lunch!

When you sit down to talk with someone one on one when you are in the 'getting-to-know-you' phase, it's a lot of back and forth with questions. "Do you like this?" or "Have you ever tried that?" So sure, you can sit and *interview* your character but sometimes that does not come off sounding natural. In the case of interviewing someone, it is just one person that you are trying to get information on.

With the classic interview format, you tend to find generic questions like "What's your favorite color?" or "Where did you grow up?" We want to dig a little deeper than that.

By this point in our workbook, you should know your main character very well. You know about their background, their family, what they look like and some personality traits. But now it's time to really let us get to know them by having an informal conversation with them.

How do you do that? Well, you have to be creative – which should be no trouble for any of you because you are creative writers! What I mean by creative is not just in the questions that you choose to ask but also in the way that you write them out and present them.

Just like in your regular writing and telling of a story, you need to grab the reader. So just listing the questions and answers is not really what we're looking for. Imagine that you are going to be submitting this conversation to a newspaper or a magazine. You'd want it to be interesting, right? You would want the reader to have enough insight into your story's character that they would want to read your book, right?

©2011 Stacey Cotrufo

Developing Your Character					Lesson Ten – pg. 55

The following are the first two paragraphs from an interview with actor Tom Hanks from Oprah Winfrey's magazine, "O".

We know Tom Hanks as the actor's actor whose portrayals often make us reconsider our own moral choices. Whether he's playing a captain on a military mission or a lover with a breaking heart, we think about what we would do—and have done. We also know Hanks as the consummate family man, a dedicated husband and father whose stirring post-award speeches about his wife, Rita Wilson, leave us reaching for Kleenex.

Hanks's roles are unforgettable. His astronomical hits include Splash, Big, Sleepless in Seattle, Apollo 13, Saving Private Ryan, The Green Mile, and Cast Away. At age 45, he has already won back-to-back best-actor Oscars for 1993's Philadelphia and 1994's Forrest Gump. On September 9, his newest project, Band of Brothers, a ten-part HBO miniseries he coproduced with Steven Spielberg, will tell the story of a heroic World War II army unit on D-Day.

That is a lot of information in just two paragraphs. Now, most of our characters do not have this kind of resume for us to pull from but what I am trying to show is that you need to give a little bit of an intro when writing up your final draft of the time you spend one on one with your character.

Further down in the Tom Hanks article, Oprah does turn it in to a Q&A format:

Oprah: *You've been described as the most uncommon common man anyone has ever known. Is that who you feel you are?*

Tom: *No—there isn't any great mystery about me. What I do is glamorous and has an awful lot of white-hot attention placed on it. But the actual work requires the same discipline and passion as any job you love doing, be it as a very good pipe fitter or a highly creative artist.*

©2011 Stacey Cotrufo

Developing Your Character   Lesson Ten – pg. 56

***Oprah:** When I mentioned to a few people that I was going to interview you, they said, "What a decent guy!" How close are you to that image?*

***Tom:** Pretty close. I try not to lie to people—the only way to control the way you're perceived is to tell the truth. No journalist has ever been in my house and no photographs have ever been taken of where I live. I don't parade my family out for display, which is the way it will stay. Yet I have a reputation for being cooperative with the press. That's because when I do give an interview, I'm willing to tell the truth about what I do for a living and how goofy it is sometimes—and how volatile it can also be.*

***Oprah:** The theme of this issue is success. Have you wrapped your brain around your success?*

***Tom:** No—it still takes me by surprise. When I used to come here to Chicago, for example, I could walk around and do everything I wanted. That's difficult now that I am instantly recognizable.*

But being that she had a large intro leading up to this part, it only made sense to go this way. On the other hand, Time Magazine did an interview with Governor Sarah Palin where it was written up in a more conversational, paragraph format.

Sarah Palin gives me a tour of the two shacks, starting with the sauna. "Usually you stay out there until the fish aren't hitting anymore, and then you come in," she says. "And here, especially in Native Alaskan culture, you come in and take a seat, and you sweat everything out." She asks Todd how hot it usually gets. "220 [degrees Fahrenheit] is too hot," he says. "190's good." "Too hot for me," she says. "But these guys do it. So, everybody comes in after fishing and gets buckets of water, and the steam lets you sweat everything out, and it's all guys and it's all gals. That's the tradition."

©2011 Stacey Cotrufo

Developing Your Character   Lesson Ten – pg. 57

Then she shows me the smoke shack. "This is usually the subsistence catch," she says, gesturing to the gutted, smoked fish drying in the 10:45 p.m. sun, "which means it's just going to be for personal use." Todd hands me a frozen pack of smoked salmon from a freezer. "And it's the best-tasting stuff in the world after a couple of weeks of drying. People then store it away and eat it through the winter. But they smoke it there and dry it here."

Really, there is no WRONG way to write up your interview. It's more about what you are comfortable with. However, there are some key points to writing dialogue to remember.

First, avoid continually using the phrases "He said" or "She said". Nobody just 'says' something all the time. People have emotions, facial expressions and gestures. Remember how we talked about that in lesson four (Giving your character a voice). Even if you are just having a pleasant conversation, your voice will have inflections, your face will react to the things being discussed, your hands will move, your body may fidget, you could laugh, you could cry...a conversation is rarely just about "he said, she said".

Now for the sake of this lesson, we are going to take the stance of this being a pleasant conversation between two people over lunch. Depending on the type of character you are writing about, you can have your lunch take place anywhere you like – a restaurant, the park, at home – wherever you are most comfortable.

If your story takes place a long time ago, you can either place yourself back in time or bring your character into present day and watch how they react to the different surroundings. The same goes if your story is more futuristic. Think of how you would react if you were the person that you are today and had to go back to say, 1920 for an afternoon? Think of how different everything would be! Keep that in mind wherever you place your character for the purpose of this lunch date.

©2011 Stacey Cotrufo

Developing Your Character   Lesson Ten – pg. 58

When writing your final draft and using the paragraph format, you also need to remember exactly HOW it needs to be written. Every time the conversation switches from one person to another, you need to start a new paragraph. You don't have two people speaking in the same paragraph normally. It helps the reader to be able to keep track of what is going on and who is saying what when you separate who is speaking.

Do not end each and every sentence with "he said" or "she said" – try using emotion to that. Also, if your writing is separated to show the back and forth of the conversation, you don't have to add who is speaking after each sentence spoken.

Exercise 10

I know that your character is someone that you created and to you they are fascinating. During your "lunch" with them, I want you to draw out what it is about them that you think readers will want to know the most. Come up with ten questions (any ten questions with the exception of "What is your favorite color" or "What is your favorite meal"). Try and make them interesting; the kind of questions that would really make a person think but also questions that directly pertain to them. Also, allow for your character to ask things of you – after all, this is a conversation between two people.

Really think on this and again, don't rush it. Make your questions be thought provoking for your character. For the character who meditates, ask something like what is their favorite bible verse. For the college student, ask them about their major and where they see themselves in five years. Of course, these are just suggestions but I want you to really almost challenge your character to think about their answer.

I am fine with either format you want to use to write – Q&A or paragraphs – but please keep in mind that if you use the Q&A approach, you are going to need several paragraphs to set the tone and introduce us again to your character. Personally, for this assignment, I think that the paragraph format is easier.

©2011 Stacey Cotrufo

Developing Your Character Lesson Ten – pg. 59

©2011 Stacey Cotrufo

Developing Your Character   Lesson Ten – pg. 61

Developing Your Character   Lesson Eleven – pg. 63

Character Transformation

A good fiction story will take you on a journey. Sometimes it is one person's journey, sometimes the focus is on many but at the end of it all, lives are changed. Growing up, most of our stories ended with "And they lived happily ever after" and while that kind of an ending is still a classic, the road to happily ever after normally involves a character transformation.

The dictionary defines transformation as a marked change, as in appearance or character, usually for the better. In the classic story of "Beauty and the Beast" the beast goes through two major transformations: The first is from a handsome prince into a beast which represented the state of his heart. He may have been handsome and wealthy but there was no love in his heart and so he was transformed physically in to a hairy beast. Later in the story, when he finally finds love and his heart opens up to care for and sacrifice for another person, he is transformed back in to human form and to the handsome prince.

Not all stories required such a drastic transformation. You can have something as simple as the school bully learning compassion; the shy girl learning to have confidence in herself; enemies to become friends…the possibilities are endless.

In real life, we all go through different transformation. We go from child to teen, teen to adult, single to married, student to worker, dependent to independent. So when you think of transformations for your characters, remember, they do not have to be as drastic as our friend the Beast but they do need to happen.

If your character is a quiet girl from a small town, what is it that is going to happen in her life during your story that will transform her? Will there be any kind of life-changing event that will have her changing her views or have her faith strengthened? Will the friends who thought they'd stick together through thick and thin find themselves questioning their friendship and be forced to go their separate ways?

©2011 Stacey Cotrufo

Developing Your Character   Lesson Eleven – pg. 64

Conflict and transformation help make for a compelling story and you want to make sure that you include it within your story. These are the things that move your story forward and help your character to evolve. At this point in the workshop and in your story development, you may not have a concrete ending. That's okay. But make sure that you keep the transformation in mind.

If you've ever read the Harry Potter series, you know that Harry went from a boy who had no idea that he was a wizard to being one of the strongest ones and it was his transformation in to a strong wizard that had him saving everyone from the most evil man of all. The tried and true story of good vs. evil is shown here and Harry, while always considered the good wizard, had a lot to overcome before he could go into that final battle. He grew up being raised by an aunt and uncle who hated him and made him feel like he was worthless! Imagine going from that kind of thinking in to a world where not only are you not worthless but the fate of the world rests on your skills!

Transformation.

In the teen novel "Speak", the main character has to start high school as an outcast. It seems as if the entire school hates her because she ratted out some of the most popular kids in school. But really, she was saving herself. By the end of the book (and trying not to give it all away) she will come face to face with her biggest tormentors and refuse to be picked on and belittled any more. She will in fact, speak up.

Transformation.

In "The Princess Diaries", Mia goes from being an outcast to a princess. Cinderella goes from being a lowly maid to marrying a prince. Some transformations are blazingly obvious whereas others are not. Learning to trust, learning to love, learning to be independent and not worry about what others think…those are true transformations.

©2011 Stacey Cotrufo

Developing Your Character				Lesson Eleven – pg. 65

Exercise 11
So where is your character going in your story? What changes do you have in store for them? In one paragraph, describe the person that they are in the beginning of your story. In a second paragraph, describe the person that they are going to be at the end of your story.

Once that's done, your journey to filling in all of the blank pages in between those two paragraphs begins…

_____

_____

_____

_____

_____

_____

_____

_____

_____

_____

_____

_____

Developing Your Character Lesson Eleven – pg. 66

Developing Your Character   Lesson Eleven – pg. 67

©2011 Stacey Cotrufo

Made in the USA
San Bernardino, CA
13 April 2017